THIS BOOK BELONGS TO:

_____

WELCOME TO RHODE ISLAND

Dedicated to all the explorers.

All rights reserved.
No part of this book may be reproduced in any form or by any means, electronic or mechanical, and no photocopying or recording, unless you have written permission from the author.

ISBN 978-1-958985-65-6

Text copyright © 2025 by Mimi Jones

www.joeysavestheday.com

A Mimi Book

Rhode Island's name has two possible origins. Some believe Italian explorer Giovanni da Verrazzano inspired the name in 1524 after comparing an island near Narragansett Bay to the Greek island of Rhodes. Dutch explorer Adriaen Block called it "Roodt Eylandt" (meaning "Red Island") because of its reddish clay. English settlers later adopted the name, cementing Rhode Island's historical place.

Giovanni da Verrazzano

Clay

Rhode Island was the thirteenth state to join the Union. It officially joined on May 29, 1790.

Rhode Island is bordered by just two states: Connecticut to the west and Massachusetts to the north and east. Additionally, it boasts a stunning coastline along the Atlantic Ocean to the south, featuring picturesque beaches.

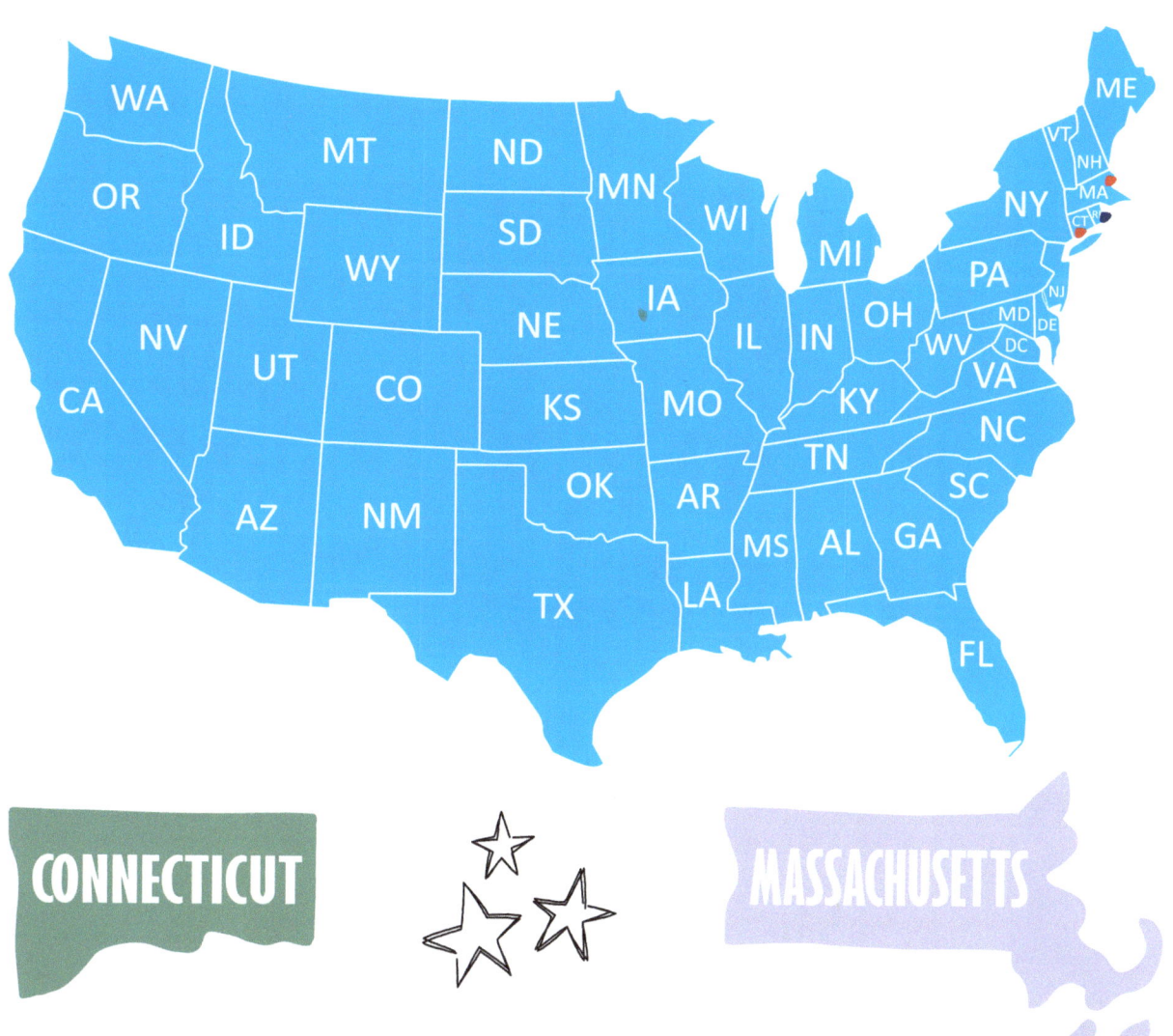

Providence is the capital of Rhode Island.
It officially became the capital in 1900.

Providence, Rhode Island, has an estimated population of about 190,790 people.

Rhode Island Capital Building

Despite its rich historical importance, Rhode Island holds the title of the smallest state in the United States in terms of land area, spanning only 1,214 square miles. This distinction places it as the fiftieth largest state overall.

There are about 1,112,300 people who live in the state of Rhode Island.

Block Island

Roger Williams founded Providence in 1636 as a haven for religious freedom.

FREEDOM

Rhode Island was the first colony to declare independence from Britain, doing so on May 4, 1776.

Rhode Island

There are 5 counties in Rhode Island.

Here is a list of them:
- Bristol
- Kent
- Newport
- Providence
- Washington

Narragansett Bay significantly shapes the geography of the state, nearly dividing it in two and featuring more than 30 islands.

The state tree of Rhode Island is the Red Maple, also known as the Acer rubrum.

On October 4, 1895, the first U.S. Open Golf Tournament took place at Newport Country Club in Newport, Rhode Island. Eleven players competed, and Horace Rawlins, a 21-year-old English golfer, won with a score of 173.

GOLF

The Rhode Island Red was named the state bird on May 3, 1954. This strong, red-feathered chicken is known for its excellent egg-laying and has been important to farming. It's a proud symbol of Rhode Island's agricultural heritage.

Rhode Island's official state fish is the striped bass. This silver fish with dark stripes is popular among anglers and plays an important role in the state's coastal waters.

The official state flower of Rhode Island is the Viola sororia, known as the Common Blue Violet. On March 11, 1968, the Rhode Island legislature officially designated the Viola sororia as the state flower.

Rhode Island has several nicknames that reflect its identity. It is commonly called the "Ocean State" because of its vast coastline and strong maritime traditions. The "Plantation State" honors its early agricultural history, while "Little Rhody" highlights its small size and tight-knit communities.

In 1774, Christopher H. Gardner, a skilled horseback performer, entertained around 3,000 spectators in Newport with trick riding and comedic acts. His venue, a riding academy called a manege, may have been America's first circus-style performance space.

The current state flag of Rhode Island was officially adopted on November 1, 1897.

Some of the crops grown in Rhode Island are apples, corn, grapes, hay, onions, and potatoes.

Some of the animals that live in Rhode Island include beavers, coyotes, deer, rabbits, and squirrels.

Rhode Island can encounter severe temperature variations throughout the year. The highest recorded temperature in the state reached 104 degrees Fahrenheit in Providence on August 2, 1975. In contrast, the coldest temperature ever documented was -28 degrees Fahrenheit (28 degrees below zero) in Richmond on January 17, 1942.

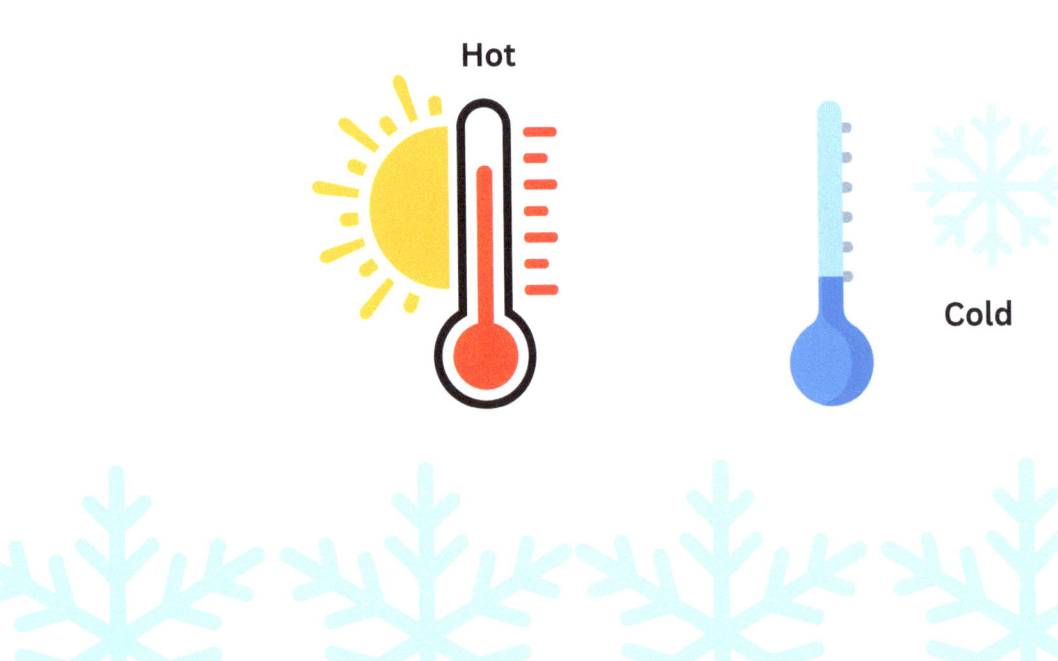

Touro Synagogue in Newport, built in 1763, is the oldest Jewish place of worship in the U.S. It symbolizes religious freedom, once welcoming Jewish families escaping persecution. In 1790, President George Washington pledged America's commitment to tolerance. Today, it remains an active synagogue and historic site.

Rhode Island's state motto is "Hope," a symbol of resilience and religious freedom since colonial times. It appears on the state seal with a golden anchor and comes from a biblical passage about hope as an anchor for the soul.

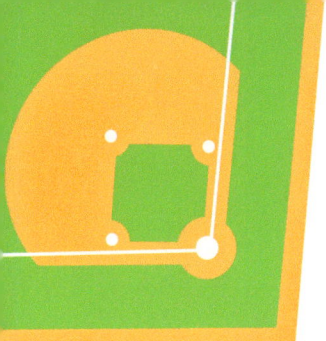  

Rhode Island doesn't have a Major League Baseball team, but the Rhode Island Rams represent the University of Rhode Island. They compete in NCAA Division I and play at Bill Beck Field in Kingston.

The Rhode Island Rams football team represents the University of Rhode Island in NCAA Division I FCS. They play at Meade Stadium in Kingston and have been competing since 1895. The team has strong rivalries with Brown University and UConn, making for exciting matchups each season.

The Battle of Rhode Island took place on August 29, 1778, during the American Revolutionary War. American forces, led by General John Sullivan, tried to reclaim Newport from the British, but after French naval support withdrew, the Americans had to retreat. Though the battle was inconclusive, it was significant for the 1st Rhode Island Regiment, one of the first racially integrated military units in U.S. history.

Beavertail Lighthouse, built in 1749, is one of the oldest lighthouses in the U.S., marking the entrance to Narragansett Bay. Located in Beavertail State Park in Jamestown, it has guided ships for centuries and survived storms, fires, and even destruction during the American Revolution. Today, it offers stunning coastal views and a museum showcasing its maritime history.

Can you name these?

I hope you enjoyed learning about Rhode Island.

To explore fun facts about the other 49 states, visit my website at www.joeysavestheday.com. You'll also find a wide variety of homeschool resources to support joyful learning at home. If you enjoyed this book, I would be grateful if you left a review. Your feedback truly helps. Thank you for your support!

Check out these other interesting books in the 50 States Fact Books Series!

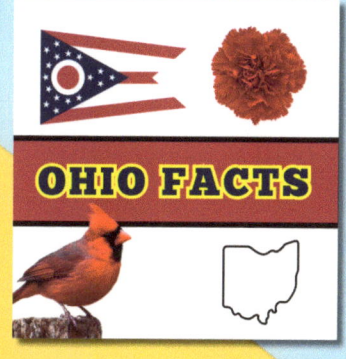

www.mimibooks.com

www.ingramcontent.com/pod-product-compliance
Lightning Source LLC
Chambersburg PA
CBHW040028050426
42453CB00002B/42